Into the Arms of Pushkin

POEMS OF ST. PETERSBURG

CAROL V. DAVIS

Truman State University Press
New Odyssey Series

Published by Truman State University Press, Kirksville, Missouri
tsup.truman.edu
© 2007 Carol V. Davis
New Odyssey Series
All rights reserved

Cover art: Sergei I. Smirnov, *Warm April*. 2003, oil on canvas. Used by
permission of the artist.

Cover design: Teresa Wheeler
Type: Minion Pro, copyright Adobe Systems Inc.
Printed by Thomson-Shore, Dexter, Michigan USA

Library of Congress Cataloging-in-Publication Data
Davis, Carol V.
    Into the arms of Pushkin : poems of St. Petersburg / Carol V. Davis.
        p. cm. — (New odyssey series)
    ISBN: 978-1-931112-70-3 (alk. paper)
    ISBN: 1-931112-71-0 (pbk. : alk. paper)
    I. Title. II. Series.
    PS3604.A9558I58 2007
    811'.6—dc22

                                                                      2007022057

No part of this work may be reproduced or transmitted in any format by any
means without written permission from the publisher.

The paper in this publication meets the minimum requirements of the
American National Standard for Information Sciences—Permanence of Paper
for Printed Library Materials, ANSI Z39.48-1992.

S/Keen

Into the Arms of Pushkin

WINNER OF THE
2007 T. S. ELIOT PRIZE

The T. S. Eliot Prize for Poetry is an annual award sponsored by Truman State University Press for the best unpublished book-length collection of poetry in English, in honor of native Missourian T. S. Eliot's considerable intellectual and artistic legacy.

Judge for 2007: Alberto Rios

for this city and its people

Contents

IV

Acknowledgments

ArtLife	"Seasons"; "Summer in St. Petersburg"
Askew	"Light"
Bluestone Review	"Jars of Pickles, Jars of Beets"
Bridges	"Choral Synagogue I"; "Choral Synagogue II"
California Quarterly	"In Translation"
Cairn	"If Now as I Wait"; "The Exotic: What the Locals Eat"
Caprice	"The Hours Between Hours"
City Works	"Are You Ever Going Back to Russia"; "Language"; "The Poplars of St. Petersburg"
Cyphers	"Are You Ever Going Back to Russia"
Ekphrasis	"The Violin Teacher Conducts Shostakovich"
Half Tones to Jubilee	"The Violin Teacher Plays Bach"
Janus Head	"The Violin Teacher Comes for a Lesson"; "The Violin Teacher Gives a Lesson in How to Sing"; "The Violin Teacher on Tour: Russia to Italy"
The MacGuffin	"Day Trip to Novgorod"; "The Prison of Crosses"
Nimrod	"Birding"; "Naming"
Poetry Scotland	"The Violin Teacher Returns Empty-Handed"
Rattle	"Salt"
The Refined Savage	"Crowded Prison Turns to Tourism to Fill Its Coffers"
Roanoke Review	"Cleaning the Graves: Bolsheokhtinskoye Cemetery"
Shirim	"Seasons"; "Teaching Holocaust Literature and Living Across from the Prison of

	Crosses"; "The Choral Synagogue I"; "Living in Another Language – I (Winter)"
Solo	"For the Man Who is Not My Lover"
Solo Café 1	"Fairy Tale"
Sow's Ear	"Dreaming of Vegetables"
The Stinging Fly	"Buying Seeds in the Snow"
Water-Stone	"The Summer Gardens"
West 47, Cuirt Journal (Galway)	"The First Nights in St. Petersburg"
It's Time To Talk About... (bilingual)	"The Violin Teacher"; "The Violin Teacher Imagines"; "The Hours Between Hours"
The Violin Teacher (chapbook)	poems in section II

"The Violin Teacher Plays Bach" won the Half Tones to Jubilee Poetry Award. "The Poplars of St. Petersburg" received the Ada Sanderson Memorial Award, Poetry Society of Virginia. "Are you ever going back to Russia"; "Language"; "The Poplars of St. Petersburg" won the City Works Poetry Award.

Thank you to the Virginia Center for the Creative Arts for residencies. I am grateful to the Barbara Deming Memorial Fund, Inc./Money for Women for a grant to go to Russia to work on this manuscript. I am deeply indebted to the J. William Fulbright Foreign Scholarship Board for grants to teach in Russia in 1996/97 and 2005 and to the Fulbright Program in Russia. Your faith in me made this book possible. Thank you to the Bureau of Educational and Cultural Affairs of the U.S. State Department and the Public Affairs Section of the U.S. Consulate in St. Petersburg, as well as to the Center for the International Exchange of Scholars; to Petersburg Institute for Jewish Studies and St. Petersburg State University; to friends in Russia and the United States; and to Hannah, Jacob, and David for coming with me to Russia for the adventure. Much gratitude to Brigit Pegeen Kelly for her astute comments on the manuscript.

I

The First Nights in St. Petersburg

I can tell you what is different, what the same.
Bananas are also imported, sold on street
corners and given over like bunches of small balloons.

The butter sliced here from a huge slab
into chunks of broken iceberg.
I remember pools of it formed after long dinners

in the heat of Indian summer at home.
Too tired to clean up, too hot for love.
From my apartment window

I see more windows.
A grandfather drinks tea
at a kitchen table.

Jars of homemade pickles
readied for winter line the sills.
In the courtyard, cats

scavenge for food.
I want you to know what it is
to stumble in another language,

where effort is weighed against
outcome like spoons of sugar.
Shopkeepers smile secretly

at one another in recognition.
An old woman asks sweetly,
Are these your children?

Her voice slides into rebuke
when I fail to understand.
It is then I hurry to enclose

my children set adrift in the unknown.

Living in Another Language I (Winter)

Light shrinks daily.
One morning the sky an expectant
lavender, the next a gray purple
of daylight unopened.
The children leave in the dark,
return in the dark.
The season for hoarding.

I have begun to stockpile
words, scrawl them on scraps
of paper, stitch them into phrases,
collected six at a time to sew
into skirt hems, inside lace blouses
patterned with vines and repetitious suns
unknown in the winter of this climate.

I could be my grandmother
Anna and her mother, Yocheved,
midwife of the Bible, rescuer of
Jewish children at the time of Moses.
The reach into jar-bottom for
the few kopecks saved in the
years before the Revolution.

Yocheved snips a thread
to separate cloth from lining.
If there even was protection
in the coats where all hope lay.
Later the sea carried Anna
to America, away from her mother
with a finality unimaginable.

Now back to live in her
city, its name restored.
My children stare at the tsar
shrouded on horseback.
They are not unhappy.
Language incidental as long as
I buy the poppy seed buns they
have come to expect daily.

I spill into the crowded
streets, know to avoid the eyes
of gypsies who circle the block
in packs of four or five.
Colorful chiffon skirts contrast
to the muddy streets, pants
of black and more black.

Still it is not enough that
the padded women who ladle
pungent sour cream into any
glass jars thrust at them no longer
wink to each other beneath their
gold-threaded kerchiefs.

I want you to know what it is
to live without language, where
extracting each word is painstaking
as the selection of 8,000 ruble mandarins
sold on every street corner with
shiny persimmons, a color
unnatural even to my California eye.

Before bed I choose the words
I will need for the next morning, lay them
on the desk chair with the folded clothes.

How without, I will sit with my friend
in the dark car speeding over the canals
in the ever-present snow, the dictionary
on my lap, unopened, useless.

Dreaming of Vegetables

I dreamed of vegetables
the year I lived in the far north,
　　　anything with crunch and texture.
At first the images were black and white.
　　　Broccoli upright on shelves like mannequin heads
with curly hair atop slender necks.
　　　Chinese pea pods floating
in the bathtub with my wash.
　　　As the days shortened and the sun
faded to a puddle of dirty snow, my dreams
　　　shifted to color.
A salad of tomatoes, yellow peppers,
　　　romaine torn like rags and radicchio,
streaked purple spilling over a glass bowl.
　　　Each shade vibrant as crayons.
I tried to pluck one of those chunks of tomato
　　　but it stuck fast to the apron of lettuce
like a snail trailing slime.
　　　I couldn't budge that juicy quarter moon
though all night my fingers struggled with it,
　　　as my jaw cranked open and shut like a gate.
In morning when I finally opened my eyes
　　　to the windowsill across the gully, there stood
the same dusty jars I had seen all year,
　　　each bursting with pickles, cabbage, and rot.

Light

In a light rain one night
in a neighborhood brimming with uncertainty
I stumble into a man on a canal bridge in
the maze of bridges weaving around St. Isaac's.
I recognize him as *fear*.
He could have been a dybbuk*
tugging at a Chassidic soul, but
that was another century
and Jews were restricted from residence.
Now he is stripped to pure form.

Leaves circle the trees
outside my window, sucking in, exhaling.
In the glare of street lights, their own sharp
yellow lasts only days before collapsing
to the orange of burnt peppers.
Pushkin's statue in the square
old and ill in his frozen youth.

Down the four steps of the shop
with the tin bucket of stinking herring
where I buy eggs loose in a bag
and the same three men line up for vodka,
longing stares from behind the counter
dressed in mismatched skirt and sweater.
She counts out the change.
I translate in my head.

Even my body, collarbone
to lip of breast, the smooth
slide to ribs becomes shadow

in the diminishing light
as *loss* perches on the kitchen counter
watching the steam rise
from pans of boiling water.
Nothing left to startle in
the darkening morning hours.

* In Jewish folklore, an evil spirit of a dead person that enters and
controls a living person's body.

Need

I have been thinking how the body
is a vulture—all avarice and need.
How longing creeps up, stalking
for days, catches with such force
it leaves you breathless.
It doesn't matter witnesses remain
offering explanation.

One month since I arrived
in this city of water and fading light
where the wind slaps between decrepit
palaces lining the canals and everyone
eats ice cream even on the coldest days.

It's true I can get by now.
The bakery clerks no longer
call out counter-lady to cashier
(louder than necessary)
as if poor language skills
were a handicap like deafness.
Maybe they're right;
it's easier to swallow
the sentences than to pull
them out like an old rag
caught in the gullet of a heron.

If taste on the tongue
cannot be verbalized,
how can a woman differentiate
between dozens of pickles

displayed at Kuznetchny Market,
the purveyors chanting,
Try this. Sweet. Crunchy.
All you could hope for.

In Translation

        The struggle
of language weaves a net
between us where a clash
of cultures, burden of
families, enticement of risk
and fear are stuck upright
like the small red flags
planted in lawns when
this city was still Leningrad
and November 5th was still a
celebration for the Revolution.
        Words, methodical
as a rolled ball between toddlers,
idioms squeezed through a sieve.
The choice of language tossed
back and forth switches midthought,
Russian to English and back.
        The air takes
on form, stiffening as a shirt
on a clothesline in an
unexpected midafternoon freeze.
        October in St. Petersburg.
Snow grows underfoot. Pedestrians
deny its existence, for acknowledgment
would prolong a winter we know
will last until May.
        All dialogue a translation,
definitions listed one to ten, meanings
obscuring into a screen between us,
where want becomes need, and need, hunger.
        Phrases strung like food.
You can almost taste the shashlik,
scorch of lamb.

The memory of sacrifices
slaps you the moment you step foot
from Mayakovsky Metro. Grease
mixing with frozen breath, a crowd
thickening on Nevsky Prospekt
like a sauce of blood and wine
in the pan, or the congealing
of fat on the plate, as if the cells
could multiply as we watch
and they do. They do.

Jars of Pickles, Jars of Beets

The days grow shorter.
I wait for a man I barely know
to return from a place I've never been.
He returns home to Russia.
Two months into my stay
and I no longer know how
to form the words
this is my home
in any language.
Mornings so dark now
the shadow of Pushkin
lengthens at 8 AM.
An arc of lamps shields
the park from our stone-
carved building.
Light diffused even midday.
They say snow is coming,
like an ache in a farmer's joints
as he turns to his wife of forty years,
It'll rain today. I can feel it in my bones.
At night I dream a caress
sweeps my back.
I turn toward this tenderness
but it is only a shudder of music
from the apartment across
the courtyard windows lined
jars of pickles, jars of beets.

The Hours Between Hours

—for E.L.

1.

In the hours between hours
when the late afternoon light settles on the air
like a vapor and drifts onto the newly painted
palaces and bridges, wraps itself on the cupolas
and vanishes heaven-bound

we drive. Only this city I know underground,
transpire through the bowels between one
metro stop and another, but on the streets
am blind as a vole groping in the harsh sunlight.
I have waited weeks

for this friendship to break open,
exposed as the brashly displayed pomegranates
in Kuznetchny Market. At the Hermitage,
awkward as crabs free from their shells,
we get out and walk beneath huge statues

of naked men holding up the world.
The words stumble over one another,
this husband loves more than ever
but it is not returned, that wife questions
the very notion of marriage, why passion

dies like a fruit abandoned on the vine.
What women talk about in undertones
the color of seabed dwelling fish.
Envious (in abstract) of a long marriage,
the comfort of sentences finished.

2.

A relationship can dive underground,
live out its usefulness and pass away
quietly like some furrowing animal who
one day turns in a tunnel, curls up, and dies.
The bones brittle, disintegrating,

found by a child bound tightly in striped
wools, sent out of doors in the last days
before snowfall. He cups them in mittened
palms, with a tenderness he will show years
later to a woman with a cascade of curls;

carries them into the warm house, as if
the bones were a body still, surrounded
by tissue and fur, the rapidly beating heart
of a frightened animal; displays them proudly
on a wooden shelf reserved for sacred treasures.

3.

I have been thinking, what we choose to reveal:
how in editing a life you can recreate it, bring
back the lover, without the weeks between
phone calls, the uncertainty of the next meeting;
transform the husband to the most

attentive and satisfying of partners,
repair between the fallen stitches before
they widen beyond the meager skills,
making a choice before it makes itself
and you left only to watch while the crevice

takes on a life of its own: breathing, giving
orders, like the idols in the shop of Abraham's
father, waiting to be smashed in the

indignation of righteousness. As if in
middle age we can summon up such strength,

grateful as we are for the light brush on
the cheek, women mostly transparent,
sexless (on the street, at the party) and
in the stagnation of a thirty-year marriage
or the friend's marriage veering off track,

between launching the children into school,
the gnawing teeth of growing debt,
not enough work to pay the medical bills,
the chronic illnesses. The days continue
without preference, years multiply, until

either the marriage becomes an independent
figure, moves in with the two like a third
partner, or one mother takes herself
and the young children a continent away,
though no one believes this were possible

or she brave enough to carry it through.
She makes the new friend in a language
so difficult for her that the friend asks,
Is it just the language or is it hard to open up?
Timing essential:

revelations too early tear friendship apart
like placing the small animal in the path
of big dogs knowingly or opening up the chest
and leaving the heart exposed. You learn
to trust and it is taken away or you say,

This is what I did. There are no regrets.
But the revelation is to the friend,

not the husband left behind. It is easier
to be the one to go, she recognizes that now.
The letters from home thinning with a

note of desperation. Her mild flirtation
with another man not revealed, how
her friends at home would say she was
not the type, as if a woman graying,
belly soft, were not capable. Or is it just

these women are without opportunity?
In the late fall of St. Petersburg, bodies
fade in the dimming afternoon light,
slip behind the statues of literary figures
who died young: manly, sanctified.

The women never deified, their sexuality
not revered. But these two women met,
talked in a light rain, will talk again,
perhaps tell their secrets. One woman places
a few small anecdotes like a bowl of salt,

a loaf of bread. She waits for the friend
to pick up the offering in hands pulled
fifty years before to the safety of evacuation
in the warmth of melons and persimmons
during the nine-hundred-day siege. She wishes

to cup them now too, to repair the world
in the dictates of the Torah.

For the Man Who Is Not My Lover

If we can dissect desire: put it in
proper form, deposit longing in the
introduction as a noun, the verb
follows active or passive; the objects
easily identified (ourselves).
Complications surround us:
separation from a wife,
but without finality, a husband
on the other side of the moon;
dependent children, both grown
and too small to understand.
If months of winter stretched
through days begun in darkness
and returned midafternoon
the same, the few hours of light
cupped in walls of snow
pushed to one side of the road.
The predictability of patterned life:
a boy's violin lessons twice weekly,
the woman's teaching schedule.
Lines must be skipped for
what remains unresolved:
marriages, the inevitable
separation at year's end.
And if, at conclusion, the eye
automatically returns to the
introductory sentence, inserting
tenderness to its rightful position
between us, we return finally
to the beginning, where we belong.

Day Trip to Novgorod

1.

On a late April morning when the gray haze
rises from the Neva River, laces through
the canals like a ballet ribbon,
weaves around the cupolas pressing its gloom
against St. Petersburg, city built foolishly on
swamp and marshland, I stroke my children awake,
then herd them into the cold.

We board a local bus out of the city.
Its translucent curtains, the color
of a tenuous spring, rise and fall
like new leaves breathing.
We roll past a dacha famous for shutters
carved with snowflakes, a yellow rarely
seen in the skies of northern Russia.

Piles of snow line the highway in metered
regularity glistening like ghostly lampposts.
We feel our position precarious, the only
foreigners on a bus lurching into
the vast countryside. I pat my pocket
for the reassurance of passport and papers.

2.

At our destination the passengers scatter
with their bundles like mice on a mission,
a packet of Indian tea, swollen cabbages,
lumber strapped by linden bark.
Only we linger, pitched on the edge
in the frailty of otherness.
I grasp the children's hands too tightly.

Did I tell you this city is so ancient
its language oozes out of the dark soil,
manuscripts written on birch bark?
Here the first pavements made of wood.
The oldest of surviving citadels;
decorated with towers and belfries,
Novgorod, first capital of the Russian state.

Never have I seen so many domes:
silver mushrooms sprout atop each church.
Approaching a twelfth century monastery
a quiet descends, even over the children, as if
the surrounding dead could be woken by their laughter.
A small dog follows us, wagging for food.
Outstretched palms appear
by the church entrance, heads wrapped
in bright floral scarves, eyes straight ahead.

Pushing on the solid door, we lean against
a carving of the Descent into Hell.
Disembodied creatures in the form of angels
hold spheres inscribed with the words
happiness, truth, love, wisdom.
In the pit below, long spears plunge
into demons with their own inscriptions
bitterness, despair, grief.

We enter as the priest circles with swaying
incense burner, the hall filling with smoke.
Our eyes struggle in the dim light of a few
slim tapers dripping hot wax before an icon
of the Savior. Opaque brownish flesh, the intense
cinnabar in the outline of nose and lips.

A cluster of old women cross themselves
right to left in the Orthodox tradition.
From this intrusion into intimacy,
where surely we as Jews do not belong,
we bow out slowly, relieved to trample
grass fertilized by centuries-old blood.
The courtyard where hundreds were slaughtered.
Here the twelfth century is as remembered as the twentieth.

    3.

We are the only tourists visible
in this timeless crevice between seasons.
The caretaker at the Vitoslavitsy Museum
of Wooden Architecture dozes at her kiosk,
unaware until the children's titters wake her.
The sixteenth century scales of these wooden walls
shimmer and a small second-story window flaps
gill-like in the cold breeze.

We duck inside, even the children's heads
would knock against the door frame.
My five-year-old lifts a wooden ladle,
begins to stir slowly in an iron pot
rounder than her belly.

We can almost smell the sulfur
of the cabbage dissolving in the borscht,
believe the steam to be rising.
We mount the stairs, dragging our feet,
eager to burrow under the straw
to sleep our way forwards and back.

If Now as I Wait for Your Call

you instead climb the three
flights of broken stairs,
careful to avoid the drip
of corroded pipe, a small
lake forming on the ground
floor of this building
slapped together between
the wars in uncertain urgency.
Streets still cling to their
Soviet names in a display
of foolish loyalty.
If as I open the door
you empty your pockets
of keys and broken strings:
leavings of a life undecided
trailing behind you like
musicians shuffling off stage
in the Unfinished Symphony.
And if in the dusk of entryway
your hand reaches for me
with the familiarity of dream
I would understand you at last
without burden of translation,
no longer dependent on the
intercession of angels.

Language

—a year in Russia

You could say that *language* has become the third party,
in the same way the sky-blue Rambler a high school
boyfriend drove the night I necked with the lure of
after-dark danger, became a fixture in that story. More

important than his tongue exploring the inside of my mouth.
That, being the first time, I wasn't sure how I felt about it.
Not absurd as the two dictionaries that follow us now
like compulsive puppies, languages reversed, like a basset

hound with tail leading, head dragging behind. If I had
married young (like the women here), I could have a teenager
of my own, could stay up late in indulgent worry. Instead,
on an eighteen-hour flight, with my three young children
　　　packed

around me like ice, I came to Russia, in what you could
call a kind of translation. A year later, comments still rise
on the street like the smell of yeast, *Look, a woman with
three children.* And the label foreigner I am unable to shake.

In this relationship, we switch off between languages,
like a child hopping on and off a bicycle, stumbling even
over phrases we claim as our own. Is it all anticipation?
For the hand to trace the vertebrae top to bottom

in a spiral, like links soldered in a silver bracelet.
Or the moment when a needed word cannot be
retrieved and we turn to face the language that
stands stiffly between us like a chaperon, and hated

as fiercely. As if such manifestations were possible
for Jews, brought up on either side of the world
in a scramble of diluted traditions. Still, we
remember when God appeared to Moses

as a burning bush. And we know it as truth.

The Fisherman and the Golden Fish

Because I have settled in the far north of Russia
where the snow itself breathes in the absence
of any real plant life and drifts grow
from the pavement like cells multiplying,

it is late April and still no sign of thaw.
The city's only color—green swirls
in the gauze skirts of gypsies who jostle
for money at the doorway of Finland Station,
where Lenin still scowls at the people in line,
waiting … always waiting.

To escape the dreariness, my six-year-old and I
join the Saturday throngs on the sagging metro,
exit at the station that collapsed into the oozing earth,
where the bones of countless peasants lie.
Then board a bus to the next station,
as accepting of this fate as any Russian.

We trudge on to the Pushkin Children's Theater.
The air heavy with unwashed wool and mud-caked boots.
Where once Young Pioneers waved small red flags
in the years before perestroika, now the empty plaza
planted with the grey slush that carpets
the streets for months at a time.

Every day I write lists of words I don't know,
tear them into scraps, thrust them under my tongue
for safekeeping, until they spill over my body,
coating my limbs like shimmering scales.

The curtain opens and women in blue
flutter chiffon scarves. Sway of their torsos,

the in and out of waves. Lulled by the rhythm,
we can almost taste the spray, feel the warmth,
now as foreign to us Californians as we
ourselves are here to the native born.

The fisherman casts his net on the water
and it expands with sea slime, while a swell
of violins imitate the metronome of the waves.
Again he casts and the strings tumble with seaweed.
I watch my daughter for signs of confusion.
Instead her face fills slowly with pleasure.

Casting a third time, he pulls in a golden fish
that begs for freedom, promising to grant his wish.
The fisherman untangles her from the meshes,
releases her with a gentleness unknown in his life.
Returning to his wife, he explains the great wonder,
The golden fish speaks our language!

*This worthless bundle of rags could not
be my husband,* the wife thinks in kind.
Her screams darken the air into a swarm of locusts.
The story familiar: the greedy old wife
scolding her husband's foolishness.

My daughter, oblivious to her poor
comprehension, clings to this story,
eagerly embracing an impossible reality.
Seduced by the fishwife's new
sable-trimmed jacket, the brocaded dress
heavy with pearls. Yet she pities the old man
who succumbs to his wife's demands.
As I do, if only in this life.

Buying Seeds in the Snow

From a cramped apartment
facing a centuries-old prison, I glimpse molars
of ice floating on the Neva. The 300-plus bridges
stretch like wire braces across the tongue of the river.
Each one decorated: here an imperial eagle guards
the once sacred water as dreary barges drag their cargo,
there chipped spirals lace through a golden rococo wreath.
Like a peasant wrapping her feet in strips of muslin,
I prepare for the frozen onslaught, bind my body
for warmth, lean into the cold, then down the vertical
escalator into the bowels of the metro.
A smell of damp wool and tired scarves hover
in the cars' air like leering dybbuks.
After two stops, the pulsating crowd
thrusts me into the unmerciful snow.
I awaken into a snaking line at one of the kiosks
that hugs the walls at Pushkinskaya Metro,
a mollusk clinging to a ship without reason.
Each pedestrian burdened by frayed bags
of potatoes and cabbages, in a Russian winter
without promise of end, where the words March
and April no longer synonyms for spring.
A gray stupor hangs over the city
a muffled excuse for the decay.
The tsar's palaces rendered mute.
I stand motionless, until racks of seeds call out
in seductive brilliance, promises of red, pink,
even an outrage of orange. And like the gray-coated
in front of me, cry, *Me too! Me too!* shoving fistfuls
of worthless rubles through an ever shrinking window.

Phone Line

What still surprises her after a year in Russia
are the phone calls that begin after 11 PM and

continue in a frenzied staccato until after 12.
When in America at this hour, a married couple

who barely talk, relying on the facileness of electronics,
turn from each other, here the socializing begins. She

wonders who will make the call; the small distance
between them: four metro stops, a few kilometers walk.

Tonight in the middle of a conversation punctuated by
short pauses to look up an unknown word, a gap opens

up. As if he were onstage at Shostakovich Hall playing
a violin concerto and in the middle of the twenty-eighth bar

of the Largo, he stops. The orchestra surrounding him
stops. The conductor no longer flutters his arms and

silence widens like the crack of an enormous
pomegranate in slow motion. If anticipation can be as

painful as loss itself, this is the moment it begins:
leaning towards the inevitable like pressing against a

storm, when she will return to America and he stays here,
bound to what they resist: unresolved marriages, jobs real

and imagined, children grown and still dependent, others,
young and unsuspecting. When all that stretches between

them is a phone line (often inexplicably dead), tying one neighborhood of St. Petersburg to another.

Living in Another Language II (Summer)

Because I have moved halfway across the world
to live in a language where, even after a year,
I am still a stranger, when I duck into a shop
my accent is instantly recognizable as foreign.
I brace for the flatness of incomprehension
as I ask for ten eggs, a jar of blackcurrant jam.

An open palm of rubles exchanged for
chocolate through the narrow kiosk window.
Behind me emptied bottles clink.
The late June sky dims
at 3 AM in a nod towards night,
like the remembrance of a face
or a slight bow to an acquaintance
passed on the Griboyedov Canal.

I wait for a man who is not calling.
My dictionary on the kitchen table
eager to translate between us.
As if it could extract each word, string them
into stability, unlike my daughter's necklace
now unraveling in front of me.
Translucent ginkgo leaves roll boldly
onto the stained oilcloth, the red any-flowers
sliding quietly, while the white beads,
round in complacence, await instructions.

II

The Violin Teacher

I am watching a man
I have just met trace
a sliver of moon between
neck and collarbone
on my child. He repeats
the action and the moon
thickens on the flesh of
this boy not far sprung from
babyhood. My middle child
(how I worry) his compliance
so like my own childhood
grounded in obedience
and torture from a pack
of older boys up the block.
Now the violin teacher holds up
his arm at a right angle and my
son follows. I half expect them
to slide off in a minuet in this
pre-Revolutionary living room
better suited to literary soirees
than my stack of abandoned suitcases.
They stop at the clothesline
stretched between cabinet
and heater and the violin teacher
strokes his fingers to demonstrate
the ease of bow across strings.
Now he picks up the violin and
begins to throw stars across
the room as the first notes of
Brahms fling towards the
endless ceiling. This vast room
devoid of personality or possessions

grows small, too small as the notes
crowd and stack like memories.
It must be I have always lived
in St. Petersburg in an apartment
with floating lace curtains
while the wind whips in from
the Gulf of Finland and the
leaves turn yellow to red.

The Violin Teacher Comes for a Lesson

Buzz and slam of grated gate four flights down.
His footsteps (I now recognize) on the stairs
the final stamping to shed ice and debris.
Pyramids of snow line the streets, pushed
into formation by women in orange vests and
shaggy wool leggings. The delicacy of their bound twigs
no match for the brutality of a St. Petersburg winter.
I open the first of double doors, pause before the second.
I have been scolded for being too quick.
He enters, dismantles fur hat, then coat and heavy boots.
I watch, hungry and shy, as if for the first time.
This is how the lesson begins, the shape of it
contained in these rituals, the stutter of two languages
colliding, where one sentence is begun in Russian by one,
finished in English by the other, then reversed.
An elaborate dance, as if a line of couples face
one another, all anticipation, while in the background
the violins no match for the rustle of stiff silk and organza.
The couples nod to one another, never crossing from the
    formal
to the familiar, as if a brush of the hand to the nape of the
    neck,
any movement not choreographed, too dangerous.
I sit back now, teacher and student in their own procession
of order, circle one another, like prey, like boxers.
Teacher places student's fingers on the bridge and bow,
then steps back to watch his invention.
The two of us look at one another without speaking,
hold our breath as a tail of notes emerges
from the bowels of the violin, pauses
a moment midair then takes flight.

The Violin Teacher Gives a Lesson in How to Sing

I take his voice, not knowing
if the words will trip, hesitant
as a toy coil on stairs, in his
language or mine.
Internalize it, play it back.
Even when the teacher explains
how the student must imagine the note:
hold it under the tongue like a magic stone
then widen the mouth and let it go.
There is the moment when the cage
door is opened before the bird flies out.
It knows its life is about to change
as yours is, when the mold of the canary's
feathers leaves the pillow of your palm
when the note is released without a waver
and the prayer drifting or steady
rises from your lips to God's ear.

The Violin Teacher Plays Bach

First an explanation
for his restless student. As the mouth shapes
into words, vowels lean on consonants, press
tightly, knocking over each other like dominoes.
Syllables drop at his feet in the confusion of
multiple languages: English for the student,
Russian between us. A triangle of anticipation
stretches like taut strings.

He picks up the violin,
eyes narrowing like the smallest crevice in
the Western Wall, where pleas, scrawled and
stuffed between stones, click in the wind.
The messages rise quickly to a slit in heaven.
Who are we to question such wisdom?

They say Bach's music
is like mathematics—all calculation and no
abandon, but as the bow slides into triplets,
gives way to trills, I think of the angels
on the ladder with Jacob. One angel stuck
his finger in the ground and a volcano erupted.

The Allegro quickens
as if in a storm, but the violin teacher's wrist
ever soft and pliant as bulrushes lakeside.
The two wives, eleven children, cows, and
sheep sent to the other side of the stream.
Jacob asleep on the rocks still.

Notes stack.
Angels perch on the ladder's rungs;
one descends and kneels.

A confusion of angles: elbows and knees
entangle in a coat of dust.
The Allegro reaches its crescendo
in the uncertainty of conclusion.
How is it that the music can end?

       The angel,
certain of defeat, touches the hollow
of Jacob's thigh and begins to sing.
The violin teacher lays down his bow
and opens his eyes.

The Violin Teacher Imagines

Even in sleep he can raise his arm
nuzzle violin under chin
shoulders relaxed, neck easy
on its axle, position his left
fingers on the strings.
He can assemble in one minute
like a half-dozing soldier leaps
to readiness and into battle.
On a late February morning
in St. Petersburg, light struggles
even as the days lengthen
in intervals small as steps.
Pedestrians pull their collars
against the wind and the ducks
appear frozen on the solid canals.
Later a ray of sun latches on a
tower of snow at the base of
Pushkin's statue, rides it like a sled
hooks onto the ice-slicked sidewalks
reflecting a mirror of harsh winter.
The violin teacher burrows deeper
under the wool and down of his bed.
He is somewhere warm.
Giant rubber plants brush their spongy
leaves against his uncovered arms.
The scent of gardenia too sweet for comfort
presses like wads of unbleached cotton
and night jasmine does not retreat
beneath the thickness of a tropical day.
A thin sheet peels down, exposing torso
to the sunlight, strong even
through a filter of white netting.

His skin, unaccustomed to nakedness,
contracts and expands in the moist air
like a heart pumping hard.
He rises, as if for the first time
as the sheet slides like oil on a bed of water.
Feet plant firmly on the cool clay tiles.
He bends slightly from the waist,
picks up the violin.
Like Adam in the Garden of Eden
without shame or pretense
he begins to play.

The Violin Teacher in Rehearsal

1.

Morning I struggle to transfer
sentences from one language to another.
You know a language when you dream in it.
In Russia my dreams all color and sound:
Martinu's Piano Quartet in bright yellow,
the resigned brown of Marin Marais' cello.
My mother dead twelve years watches,
words etched in the lost language
of her first-generation childhood.

2.

Chunks of snow fall from rooftops,
sidewalks roped off as women in orange vests
lean on long brooms to gossip and laugh.
Pedestrians cross the street to escape
the avalanche, pause in admiration at its ferocity.
Drainpipes drip razors and a boy in fur hat,
flaps wild in the wind, stops to break
icicles with his boot.

3.

All day I drift: prepare meals,
separate the children in their squabbles.
I think of you in rehearsal,
a cavernous concert hall.
Sweeping bow across violin in
the repetition towards perfection.
Later your compact hands curl and flex
for your student, arms circle him
tucking violin into nook of collarbone
like a mallard settling for the night.

4.

In the dark I picture your hands
tracing an outline of notes on my body.
Holding me in a shudder of music.
Beethoven, Shostakovich, the pull
to the baroque composers I love.
We would unearth the nucleus
of each movement, lean full force
against gravity like a Largo
dragging itself across the page,
resisting the finale.

The Violin Teacher Plays
with His Orchestra

Procession of first violinists, then second,
wind players with too little to hold in the
wings of their fingers, a burden of cellists,
bent as if the weight of their instruments
lay in full force on their backs, gaze never
lifting to the balcony, where people press
against a single row of seats.
The violinist's footsteps methodical.
He walks onstage as if in dream,
eyes focused beyond this hall—
beyond the streets muddied with snow,
sidewalks dangerous as tongues,
canals frozen and the Neva littered
with ice chunks in isolated patches
not solid in the darkness of mid-January.
The notes stream behind him like a tail,
as if he had finished and now sat slumped
in the aftermath of the Shostakovich
he is yet to play.
Where do the notes go?
Compressed in the rafters of this centuries-old
palace or crumpled into the pockets
of the men and women who come and go alone,
float down the stairs like an errant cell
in the bloodstream, and disappear into
the cavernous metro circling the city
like a noose, like a halo.

The Violin Teacher on Tour:
Russia to Italy

Last Sunday of April.
Snow falls even as the light creeps
onto the steps of the Neva Embankment
lingers in the crevices 'till after 9
motionless as the outstretched palm
of a babushka begging by the metro exit.
The violin teacher carefully folds his wool
muffler, lays his fur hat on a top shelf.
He pulls out a cotton shirt, pale as the sun
on a tile roof in northern Italy where
he will sit on church steps in a week's time
watching shadows of formless clouds
on the cobblestones as two young women
in tight skirts cross the courtyard.
Click of their heels clear as the high C
he will later play in the small concert hall.
Now squinting even in the much-loved sunlight
memory of winter, constancy of darkness
and snow, endless trips on the winding metro
to Conservatory, to the apartments
of private students, evenings in concert
at Shostakovich Hall, collapsing at home
only near the border of midnight.
He remembers and doesn't, details
fading in the drowsiness of uncounted hours.

The Violin Teacher
Returns Empty-Handed

If light and warmth could be
pocketed, folded precise as a
Bach fugue in a tight corner
of his suitcase between tuxedo
and dress shirts, the violin teacher
would bring home this priceless souvenir
from his South American tour. For in

the city of his birth, April has been a
month of monochrome. Tree branches
the color of dirt-laden screens, sky
brushed in broad strokes of gray,
the faces of pedestrians stripped
of expression, as if by paint thinner.

This northern Russian city, built
on bog and swamp, is sinking again.
Even the angels protecting corners
of crumbling apartment buildings and
palaces avert their gaze, unable to save it.

The violin teacher returns jet-lagged.
Face drawn, hands aching,
he knows he has forgotten something
that could save his life, but what?

The Violin Teacher Conducts Shostakovich's Ninth Symphony

1.

In each of the thousands of concerts
the violin teacher has played,
he has walked onstage with the full
orchestra, in a forward thrust
like a wave reaching shoreline.
All 100 musicians sit down en masse
in a sloping arc towards the sold-out hall,
then wait uneasily for the click
of the conductor's polished shoes on the
worn parquet of the pre-Revolutionary stage.

But on this late October evening,
the light of the Petersburg sky flickers
in the certainty of diminishing hours.
Momentarily a belt of snow will tighten
around the city and the dripping sun
will settle into five months of resignation,
for once winter begins, the sun loses all power.

The violin teacher waits in the wings.
His coat different tonight, tail longer,
even the cut of the satin collar.
His fingers twitch, as if already conducting,
until he wills them motionless.
The granite wall of his back has never faced
the audience as it does now in its broad silence.
His darting eyes do not still, flittering instead
from oboe to flutist, unable to search out
the reassuring nod of friends in the balcony.

The violin teacher positions himself squarely
on the riser, his arms drift up as if pushed
by hot steam. They float midair on a ribbon
of unplayed notes, for what appears
as several minutes, to the uneasy audience.
Then his forearms crash down as befits
the opening bars of a song of victory.

2.

Who is the final authority
in the revision of history?
The drone of petty bureaucrats
as noisy as an army of termites?
The historian frantic to secure
his legacy with a radical rewrite?
As now the life of Shostakovich
is revisited in the Ninth Symphony.
Which is it? A smug first movement—or
a sonata structure mocking righteousness?

Next the charge of the presto drowns out
the underlying disquiet, like the voices
in the '40s whispered in communal bathrooms,
while water poured full throttle from the tub
to thwart the metallic bugs positioned
by the men listening behind stone walls.

The fourth movement tumbles on.
Is it epic glory? Or empty rhetoric
flailing over the audience in the recitative
of an impassioned bassoon?
And the affront of the finale's trivial tune,
reinforced by absurd instruments.
For who can take seriously a tambourine,

cymbals, the lowly triangle?
A hollow victory? An ironic commentary?
Shostakovich bowing, broken, begging
for rehabilitation in a final humiliating plea?

III

Cleaning the Graves: Bolsheokhtinskoye Cemetery

They come each holiday,
peeling off tram and bus
like couples fanning apart
in a country dance, women
to the left, men to the right.

Single file through hobbled
arch into the cemetery.
Each grave enclosed by metal fence,
to prevent any escape.

One in every party carries
variations of the same:
bucket of old rags, a cracked bar
of brown soap, a bottle to fetch water.

First the gathering of leaves,
for the linden and birch shed at will,
sometimes, just to spite them.
Next the scrubbing of stone and cross.
Here lies a Hero of the Soviet People,
son at his side, a mound small
as a newborn's bassinet.

Two sisters arrive at one to stay
the afternoon, straight till lockup.
Practical women with rubber shoes,
matching sweaters, colorless
as the granite they bend over.
They work in silence, voices

saved for conversations
with their recently departed.

The grayer one brushes
the headstone in steady strokes.
Her hands remembering
the long glide of wooden comb
when her mother took down
her own hair at day's end.
And if the girl completed her tasks,
she was allowed to comb that hair
in all its golden goodness.

Mother and daughter stand
by the window as the light
disappears before them.
Window open to the brief
warmth of summer.
Or taped tight against
the deafening snow.

Now the grave digger
walks jauntily up the lane,
shovel dragging behind him.
Each path with name
mounted on a sign pole.
As if this a real street
where whispers slither around
corners, leaping over back fences.

He digs. A small hole
opens up to embrace
an ash-filled wooden box,
cradled by the old aunt born
before the Revolution, survivor

of the nine-hundred-day siege.
The affront of outliving
your entire family.

She throws dirt on the box,
the sound ringing through her body
as if she were kneeling in the
bell tower at the onslaught of chimes.
She pours a glass of vodka,
sets it at the head of the grave, a slice
of black bread carefully laid on top.

Other graves sprout plastic flowers,
a ribboned wreath, fading photos
smiling into the future.
She walks away backwards
so as not to disturb the dead.

The Summer Gardens

They said the fence was so beautiful
the terminally ill came from all over
the world to see it. Lucky, you were,
if you died near its gates.
Tall as three men standing head to head,
wrought iron filigree delicate as Belgian lace.
Even during the years of famine,
followed by the years of silence
when a man occupying the smallest corner
of a communal apartment, someone you
thought you knew well, could disappear
in the middle of the night, just like that.
A single joke murmured or even thought,
like a dirge moaned into a cup of tea, was enough.
Still the imperial eagle stood watch over the gate,
one head longing for the West, the other stoically facing East.
Encircled by pencil thin canals, saltwater tears
streaming down the face of the city,
bystander to so many deaths.
But the gardens forever a refuge, where one
marble nude gestures upward in conversation,
as if relief could be found even heavenward,
while her partner toots on a piccolo, totally self-absorbed.
Maybe distraction is a form of solace,
when the pain of witnessing too much
threatens to shut down all the parks
to silence all the music.

The Prison of Crosses

My apartment faces The Prison of Crosses.
Friends ask, *Do you know where you live?*
Older than the Revolution, the name survived
even the long years of sentences without charges,
locked cells with forgotten keys. Since
perestroika, the occupants simply felons.

Spring now, but this year in name only,
for in this month of April, no sun has
brought comfort to the still frozen ground.
The snow has melted, leaving a veneer of ice
stretched treacherously over the barren
land in front of my building. Water is trapped
under the ice and my young daughter checks
for goldfish on the way to school, certain
to spot a glimmer of thrashing golden tail.
Just once in her life I should like

to satisfy her. Instead I smile weakly,
hurry her into the thrust of pushing
crowds funneling sieve-like
into the metro turnstiles.

On Saturday nights the streets swell
like tongues with the stagger of drunken men.
After a year, I have grown used to that,
but in this new location, far from the
glamour of Nevsky Prospekt, clusters
of people gather with the thrust
of weeds pushing through the mud.

At first I thought my yard a meeting place
but then at dusk I heard a call.

Cry of unseen birds in darkened woods.
A leather-gloved hand cups around the
mauve stained lips of an elegant woman.
Misha, she cries, then a second and third time.

Not far away a partial unit of
grandmother, mother, two boys
in blue snowsuits. All begin to shout,
promise a next visit, smiling to one another.
No faces visible through the grated windows
yet these friends and families
know the precise location of their own.
And once, in the middle of the night

as snow fell on the thickly bricked prison
and smoke from the never barren chimney,
a song, a chant rose over the walls,
wafting over the Neva, out to sea.

Teaching Holocaust Literature and Living Across From the Prison of Crosses

Tonight the faithful gather under my window for the ritual
calling to brothers and lovers in the prison across the road.
Bottles of local vodka and cheap beer mount into teetering
    pyramids,
rising like campfires to light up the courtyard.
Young women in tight skirts, families without fathers,
like a missing piece in a chess set.

A forearm squeezes between grates of a blackened window.
Fingers wave foolishly, as if a story could drip from these
    hands,
catch on a gust of wind and escape over the Neva.
Ten men to a cell built for two; no visitors allowed before trial.
Held for years in this century-old prison for petty crimes
perhaps not committed.

A mid-April snow muffles the grinding of tram wheels,
the slow dragging of overloaded trucks from the antiquated
factory in a neighborhood barely afloat in this bankrupt city.
Built on the swampland of Peter the Great and the backs
of serfs dragged in from the countryside.

The Angel of Death perches on the embankment, patient,
for violence ever present in a country where the skeletons
of millions click their teeth in unmarked graves,
a reminder of a brutal history ever ready for repetition.

The Exotic: What the Locals Eat

In Russia food stores are segregated:
        eggs sold loose in a basket,
picked through, then held to the light and
        examined like rare amber; the meat stall
with the mounted steer's head leering

On my street dairy is sold from
        a blue-striped kiosk under
Lenin's fierce gaze, his arm still
        outstretched from Finland Station.
Has no one told him Communism fell?

As I buy apple and currant yogurt,
        flavors unavailable in America,
foil packages lined straight as a picket fence
        catch my eye, each the size of a squat nail.
A giraffe peers from one, koala in a eucalyptus from another.

What is this, please? I ask in halting Russian.
        The vendor shrugs her thick shoulders
as if to say, *Fool, everyone knows this delicious treat.*
        Where have you lived all your life?
She wrinkles her face like an apricot drying.

Shamed into silence I fumble for five ruble coins
        as two women behind me growl in impatience.
I snatch my purchases and slink off, while a gypsy circles
        assessing her prey; I break into a slow trot,
finally sinking onto a bench under the chattering poplars.

I unwrap the foil, take a bite of not-so-sweet chocolate.
        Hidden inside: cheese, both solid and creamy,

a candy unlike any I've ever tasted. I savor it slowly,
	until my jaw takes off in a gallop, faster and
faster, that threatens to lift from my body.

This must be the national secret, kept from me
	for a solid year, what the locals are born knowing.
All doors will open for me now in this mysterious society.
	My luck will change here, I know it.

Crowded Prison Turns to Tourism to Fill Coffers

—headline, St. Petersburg Times

They are giving tours at the Prison of Crosses.
Wake early on a Sunday morning
for the privilege of an hour-long guided tour.

For a year I witnessed the slow creak
of the enormous wooden gate jerking open
for the Friday morning deliveries.
But how much bread could the truck
bear when just 2.9 rubles (11 cents)
is spent daily on food for each prisoner?
I trudged through the litter of notes rising
above the winter snowdrifts in my courtyard,
then sinking into the spring sludge: shorthand
messages inmates blow through long cardboard pipes
to friends and relatives on the outside.
Nightly I woke to the calling of men's names
by their girlfriends perched beneath my windows,
fashionable in short skirts even at 2 AM.
The shouts reverberated off the brick walls
on either side—prison to apartment—stretching
into a web to catch the floating memories.
All that is left, a staccato of names. For no visitors
are allowed in this, Europe's largest remand prison.
A reluctant voyeur to an intimacy so private,
I clamped my ears, hid beneath
the bedsheets to escape the forced witnessing.
Towards dawn the net hardened into a cupola
crowning Komsomola Street: an artificial heaven
where it was possible for prayers to ascend and
cell doors to snap open.
Now I am back in America, fruitlessly defining

desperation: why people go to work when
no paycheck waits at week's end.
The stubbornness of loyalty. Fatalism so inbred,
a mutated gene found only in Russia.
How to coax soup enough from one pale
cabbage and a few tired potatoes.

The Honey Sirens of Kuznetchny Market

In an unmarked building next to the metro
across from St. Vladimir Cathedral with its
two imposing cupolas and walls golden as the flesh
of ripe plums stands Kuznetchny Market,
known for the freshest produce in all of St. Petersburg.
In the byways and alleys bordering it, trucks
double park and dark-haired men speaking
unfamiliar languages and puffing on hand-rolled
cigarettes unload cartons and burlap sacks.
Old women, solid as stone lions, line the steps
selling large plastic bags hanging from their arms
like cheap bracelets and emblazoned with slogans
in English and pictures of scantily clad women.
The smell of meat and blood, dirt and vegetables
recently pulled from the earth or else pickled,
wafts over us as we step onto the sawdust covered floor.
Straight ahead behind large folding tables
stand the honey sirens. They call out in Russian,
Come! Come! Sweet! Try some!
And like children answering the Pied Piper's flute,
my brood, already entranced, step up and accept
the offer of magic potions dripping from broken sticks.
They lick their lips, turning to me in full expectation.
Youngest first, eyes wide in pleading, her small hands
tugging at my coat sleeve. Next up her older brother,
a tad reserved, then finally the eldest, mouth set
in determination to best represent the cause.
They don't even much like honey and even if I'd
brought a container and had it filled, the jar
would sit unopened in the cupboard for months,
then be discarded. But none of this matters now
for the women coo seductively and my three

gladly succumb. If this were an opera, the children
would throw open their chests and sing in full bravado
or fall to a kneel, arms outstretched, but instead
all motion freezes: the pickle sellers, the butchers
with cleavers raised, the men in aprons emptying
kilos of potatoes yellow, purple,and white.
All await my answer.

The Choral Synagogue I

Surrounding the Choral Synagogue a black fence
decorated with Magen Davids,* twisting vines, Hebrew
with spaces between the letters wide enough to insert
a prayer, like the slips of paper stuck in the Western Wall
clicking in the wind like a thousand locusts or a
child's fingers dragging over a fan.

Such an oddball community here—ones left:
the fiercely committed to rebuilding Jewish
life anew, the assimilated, the old wracked
with memories of life before and during…
chief rabbi imported from New York.
And how like the Jews to have a breakaway synagogue,
even with the numbers dwindling yearly, though now
economic hardship more fearful than anti-Semitism.

Less than a month since we arrived, Rosh Hashanah.
I dress the boys in suit jackets, daughter in a fancy dress.
A long metro ride, then a bus and tram.
Prayers have already begun. We are pointed up two flights of
        stairs.
Our heels echo on the granite; how high we are in the women's
        section.
Only a dozen others—mostly old women so pleased for
        younger company.
A gnarled hand reaches out and strokes Hannah's cheek.
Panic sweeps her face and she inches closer to me.

In the sanctuary below the rabbi is chanting while two men
        confer.
The congregation rises and my eight-year-old asks why we are
        sitting
so far away, this separation of men and women foreign to him.

Go downstairs, I say and surprisingly he does,
attaching himself to a tallis-wrapped** man on the aisle.
What language will they talk in?
Or perhaps no language at all, just a hand on a shoulder,
a reverse immigration.

* star of David
**prayer shawl

The Choral Synagogue II

Next week will be Passover.
How will we observe it in a
country with few manifestations
of Jewish life left? Though two doors
from the store that sells loose eggs,
I spotted a name stenciled in Hebrew
on the window of a small market.
Excited I peeked in, but the stock
the usual assortment of tea and
chocolates, a few sad sausages,
bottles of vodka lining the wall.
Too shy to ask, I decided the owner
didn't know what the sign said.

A friend calls to say the synagogue
will have matzo.
Bring 12 rubles to pay for it, she says.
Passover always linked with rebirth,
but it's hard to think of green shoots
and renewal now when the ground
is still buried and there's no sign of spring.
The snow underfoot darkens after so many
months of winter and my children's cheeks
pale dangerously, even whiter than the
half frozen cabbages stacked in pyramids.
Finally I understand why vegetables are pickled
here, stored in glass jars on windowsills.

I take the children to school.
How pleased they are that the soccer field
was flooded and now hosts ice hockey games
with schoolmates from around the world.

Born in California, my three had never met winter.
Now they bundle beneath layers of cotton and wool
until walking itself becomes a hardship.

Off the synagogue's side entrance an open door.
A short man in a hat stands behind a
table sagging with piles of matzo
in neat rows like a checkerboard.
I recognize him from Rosh Hashanah, join the line.
How much do you want? I hold up my hands.
He squints slightly, as if counting how many
pieces would fit between the vice of my palms.
He tears some brown butcher paper, slices string
with a knife and binds the matzo with the precision
of a seasonal clerk wrapping a holiday present.
He ties it, a bow or a knot, I don't remember.

I take the package, thinking of the displays at home:
Passover chocolates, packaged soups, cakes, dish soap,
even the ridiculous and unnecessary: bubble gum.
Then over the miniature walkway past
Rimsky-Korsakov Conservatory.
Midmorning but no promise of warmth.
An unforgiving wind blows over the River Moika.
Far to the metro, but I don't want to be squeezed
on the tram like a slide under a microscope.
So I walk and walk, all the way to Sennaya Ploshad,
the square where Raskolnikov killed off the old woman.

This city is haunted. The ghosts of Pushkin and
Dostoevsky lurk beneath the grimy archways
taunting pedestrians to jump from
the bridges spanning the Neva.
No wonder alcoholism and despair wrack the city.

Even now Tchaikovsky rewrites his sextet
in the presence of Glinka and Liadov.
Fugitive notes from the Cantabile escape
museum shrines in every neighborhood.

This plaza is never empty and even now,
with the temperature dropping, old women
line the entranceway with the patience
of guests on church stairs waiting
to toss rice on a bride and groom.
They are selling stockings, slippers, handkerchiefs.
I clutch my treasure to my breast and descend
into the mouth of the metro.

IV

Stravinsky Revisits Oranienbaum

Millions of years passed
before splashing was heard
    then a scraping of scales
    and a rubbing of claws
Much later wood became flute
and cellos learned to fly
    Sound ground into steel
    on a track and hiccups of
smoke muted the glorious mustard sun
muffled the schoolyard banter
    Then eighteen years before
    one century slipped into another
Stravinsky was born near the border with Finland
The Firebird landing in Paris
    in 1910   Berlin in '12
    At the premiere of *The Rite of Spring*
howls of rage clung to the notes like parasites
The next year Stravinsky carried triumphantly
    on the shoulders of an enthusiastic—if
    somewhat fickle—audience
He thumps an E major chord with his
left hand   E flat major seventh with his right
    The bon vivant life: champagne
    with Cocteau and Gide
Popularity necessitating reinvention:
how to pull in a crowd   keep them in their seats
    Twenty voices in counterpoint
    Bitonality granting ears a choice
The arranging hand
in the quick aside of a solo
    In St. Petersburg and Moscow the circle
    of Rimsky-Korsakov dismissed *Rite*

as so much fashionable noise
Musical sequence turning Stravinsky
        away from nationalism at home
        to European modernism abroad
He stripped color believed essential
deleted whole parts of the orchestra
        as if the hand of God
        reached onto the stage
plucking out groups of instruments
entire sections of violins silenced
        like startled deer
        Composing for winds only
Standing in the back of the concert hall
in tux and tails watching the frenzy
        until after the War
        out of favor   out of fashion
An assistant restores confidence
the twelve tone period   the reputation
        And at the end the old
        Russian tone creeps back
A tour of the Soviet Union in 1962
Shock of nostalgia   throngs of admirers
        He visits the village of his birth
        not far from St. Petersburg
a torn photo of Lenin in the crumbling station
an out-of-date schedule tacked to the wall
        Deep in the forest Catherine
        the Great's secret palace
For two days she sequestered there with a lover
Its inlaid patterned floor of bleached and dark wood
        On the silk wallpaper men carry
        Chinese lanterns to light the way forward

Fairy Tale

On a rickety tram that rocks dangerously on warped tracks,
I travel out of the city, the only woman in a group of ice
fishermen. On my way to fetch my six-year-old, staying with a
schoolmate and an old woman who speaks no English. Seven
nights in the forest, my daughter's first time away. This must
be an initiation, though for whom, I don't know. I count eight
stops and prepare to depart, even before I spot the village
name beneath a shawl of snow.

Down a narrow road, past a store boarded up for winter. I
stumble on a decayed mansion rising out of scrub and slush.
Its exterior streaked with too many tears, splotched like a
face consumed with sorrow. Surely raccoons have pushed up
the floorboards. The lace of the nursery curtain now a tatter
of web. I heard the prince was a cousin of the Romanovs.
This estate his refuge from the intrigues of the court. And for
a dozen years it worked, until the fevered pitch of war and
starvation consumed the peasants and they surged over the
low stone wall to the entrance, shoving until the wood gave
way in a resounding crack.

As I pass I turn to see if the skeletal building still stands, then
round a bend to the dacha. The door with no handle gives
way easily. Inside the dim room my daughter perches on a
three-legged stool, pressing a wet rag to the forehead of the old
woman who lies feverish and flat on a narrow cot. Much later
I recount this tale of crumbling mansion, owl nests hidden
in the hollows of trees, my daughter ministering to a sick old
woman.

The Poplars of St. Petersburg

Summer delayed this year
in the far north.
Late June and only now
the poplars rip open
their winter coats
shelling the sidewalks
with puffs of white stuffing,
pookh, in Russian,
summer snow.
The balls stick in the
corner of the eye
like a memory of sleep,
or slide onto the tongue,
lodge in the gullet.
Then expand in the belly
as unsatisfying as fistfuls
of snow to the hungry
old women who shuffle
into the metro, clinging
to passageways like
mollusks to a host.
First time visitors to the city
puzzled, then charmed;
the residents tired of it
and all that clogs this city—
broken trams, hundreds of cars
slinking towards Palace Square.
And the embarrassment
of this foolishness—too many
female trees planted by Stalin.
The *pookh* exposing the sex
of it, a parody of the bodies

pressing one to the other
on overcrowded trolleys.
No attraction, only necessity,
so that the shell of boundaries
thins and wears, the coating
of anonymity over the eyes
tearing in spots, while
all around the *pookh* beckons.

Birding

Let me come back a birder.
Name with certainty that squawker
outside my kitchen window
I think is a Willow Warbler.
Next time, give me useful knowledge.
Names I can attach myself to
like the weight on a kite's tail
that keeps it from pulling
out of a child's fist in a sweep of wind.

I forgot to tell you I am back in Russia.
But I am not asking for names in both languages.
Just reassure me that the birds
swirling outside my fifth floor apartment
are indeed Common Gulls swept in
from the Baltic ahead of the approaching storm.

It is September 1st—Day of Knowledge.
The balloons tied to the lampposts declare it so.
Seven-year-olds in maroon blazers
remind me of Red-breasted Mergansers
that lost their way from Alaska
heading west across Siberia.

Opening day of the school year.
I saw a girl in a ponytail fastened by fur
fluffy as a Willow Tit.
Her mother held one hand, grandmother the other.
I thought they would lift up in a whirl of wings,
the older generations so puffed up with pride.
They crossed over the bridge of the little river
that winds near my building.

The three of them bent over the railing
to call to the ducks below.

Naming

If you denied a name to something
perhaps it would cease to exist.
—Penelope Lively

This morning a froth of clouds
floats on a stripe of blue sky.
The sunlight cuts a swath over the top half
of the grove, the bottom sunk in shadow.

A foreigner, I am suspended without language,
the word for a needed object, *twine* for example, unknown.
The futile miming while a salesclerk
scowls his impatience.

I gather up my point-and-pay purchases.
A left and two rights to get home.
Syllables leak from the plastic bag
staining the sidewalk.
I unpack, then scavenge my apartment
for words, string them across the hallway.

Soon the frost will cover everything.
The words will freeze on the clothesline,
letters missing like the names beneath
photographs mounted on the gravestones.
Eyes that reprimand the living,
taking note of the infrequency of visits.

Without words to name them
the trees lose their crisp form,
blending one into the other, a gloss
of pale green, overlapping shades,
the mottled browns.

Needle Arts

—for Anna

Needle arts are no longer taught, not in the U.S., not in Russia,
though a young American is cross-stitching her way
through villages southwest of Moscow, collecting patterns
from old women no longer needed.
On three-legged stools, they pull stubby needles
and gossip away the seasons.

A year in England, stiff backed on long wooden benches,
my classmates and I, bound at our necks by nooses
of blue and gold striped ties.
Our hands not allowed an idle minute.
Pillows, pincushions, aprons, we embroidered them all.
Spring bloomed in our hands, tulips in early April,
pearl cotton cowslips in June. We perfected a whipped stitch
of climbing roses impatient in its speed.

My daughter knows none of this, though lately she has pleaded
with me to drag out the sewing machine, covered now
in a beard of fine dust. I trust my own hands better.
Memory flows from fingertips to thread.
Wildflowers sprout from my palms.
Draw the loop up to cover the petal, thrust
the needle down to fasten it, centering the daisy's eye.
No forgiveness in the needle arts.

Salt

A man bends in the entryway of the market stalls
sprinkling salt from a box.
His boots are rubber, a green so pale
they are almost no color.
That is right because there is no sun,
no warmth this time of year.
The box of salt is also without color,
though it holds the memory of blue,
the curtain of sky over the Neva
in late spring, when couples sit
on steps of the embankment, saying little,
arms linked like the ornamental chains
of the cannons behind them.
Now the man surveys the floor, turns,
his feet sliding in a figure eight
as if skating on an indoor rink.
The salt mixes with snow and ice
riding in like parasites on the black boots
of the shoppers toting black bags already bulging.
If the door is propped open all day ice will form.
Then he will have to sprinkle more salt.
Or else stand aside to watch the women slip,
catch themselves or fall.
He will grade them on their performances
and they will receive low marks, every one of them.

The New Russia

More a wave than a drift
the flakes churn, white froth arcing
over the fierce wind.
First blizzard of the season,
though elm leaves still shine like a constellation
of yellow suns against the morning gray.
The kind of day Americans
always picture:
Snow, buildings drained of color.
Dreary grandmothers weighed
down with sacks of potatoes and beets.
It's not like that anymore.
Now the spiked heels
of young women clatter down the pavement
toward the open mouths of designer stores.
No more hooded kiosks
line the boulevards where customers bought
dark loaves cut in half and men
stood about waving beer bottles.
This is the new Russia
of suntans from Egyptian holidays,
gated houses with security cameras,
foreign cars and chauffeurs waiting at the curb.
Still when the church bells summon
the faithful and the government shuts down another
newspaper, it's hard to remember what century this is.

Are You Ever Going Back to Russia,

friends ask in a tone precise as a cut to the tongue.
The unimagined life the only one acceptable.
But I could talk about the Petersburg canals,
the seduction of them. Even the muck and filth
of the water, contaminated fish only
the starving would eat.
How the first year I shied away from the crates
fish sellers stack on street corners.
By the second I began to stroke the translucent scales,
convinced I could restore life.
Then I started to eat the nameless fish,
working my way around the bulging eyes,
down the length of the bony body.

The canals took up residence, throbbing through my veins,
careening around hipbones, lodging behind knees.
I stole their bridges; hung their ornaments in my closet
for special occasions: gold-winged sphinxes,
lions with curled manes guarding the Griboyedov Canal.
An iron-muscled boy breaks in a fiery horse
at the Anichkovsky Bridge over the Fontanka Waterway,
The double-headed eagle wings back two centuries,
through assassinations of the tsars and the city's name changes:
St. Petersburg, Petrograd, Leningrad, and back again.

I hung the wrought iron filigree of Troitsky Bridge
from my waist like a belly dancer, the carved angels
gathered up as earrings to adorn me.
If these icons could protect this city, they could save me too.
This is how it begins, even before you adopt Russia as your
    own.

The bleached bark of birches stretches along the railway to
    Moscow,
the branches wave blessings like priests swinging incense
where once mothers waved their last good-byes as sons were
    sent to gulag.
Old men trudge along the tracks trailing small carts burdened
    with potatoes.
All they need for a half year of winter. Sustenance enough for
    their beliefs and mine.

About the Author

Carol V. Davis was born in Berkeley, California, the granddaughter of Yiddish speakers from Russia/Ukraine and Germany/Austria. When she was three, her family moved to Europe where her father worked for the Marshall Plan. Trained as a dancer, she also studied Russian literature, earning her MA in Slavic languages and literatures from the University of Washington. She is the author of a full-length bilingual collection, *It's Time to Talk About...*, published in 1997 in Russia, and two chapbooks, *Letters From Prague* and *The Violin Teacher*. She was a senior Fulbright scholar in St. Petersburg, Russia, in 1996/97 and 2005. Her poetry has been read on NPR radio and on Radio Russia. She teaches at Santa Monica College, California.